SAY YES TO GOD

The Faith Journey of an Army Chaplain and Pastor

By

Rev. Donald C. Humphrey, CH Col USAR, Ret.

ISBN: 9781796541069
Imprint: Independently published

Cover photo courtesy of Billy Pasco from Unsplash

*This book is dedicated
to my beloved wife, Pat, my best friend and
helpmate for 62 years;
to my children, Connie and Donald of whom I
am so proud;
to my sister, Lilian, who encouraged me to write
this book; and
most of all to God who reached down in His
Grace
and Mercy, found an aimless man and set him
on a path of service and purpose.*

Table of Contents

Introduction

Matthew 19:26 *With God all things are possible.*

Several people have said over the years that I should write a book about my experiences, but I wasn't too enthused about it. I didn't think I had anything to say that people would want to read. However, the suggestion kept coming up. Just recently my sister Lilian encouraged me again to write about my life. I'm spending the winter with my daughter in Texas. While she's at work, I'll take the plunge into writing.

First, let me introduce myself. I've been a pastor for fifty-nine years. I have had eighteen civilian and eight military congregations. I've traveled all over the world and was married to a wonderful, supportive wife for sixty-two years. I'm retired now and my wife passed away a few months ago. I'm eighty-eight years old and hopefully still going strong. This book is about how my life changed when I said "Yes" to God.

Chapter One

The Early Years

Like Abraham Lincoln, I was born in Hodgenville, Kentucky. I was the seventh of eight children -- four boys and four girls. In order it was Evelyn, Paul, Thelma, Herman, Lilian, James, me and Yvonne. My parents were Everett and Lena Humphrey. Like I heard someone put it once, we weren't poor, we just didn't have any money. My parents were both hard-working people. They weren't well educated, but they did their best to take care of us.

My father had a variety of jobs. He was mostly a handyman. He worked at a factory when we moved to Louisville, but when I was eighteen, he had several strokes and fell and hit his head. He was unable to work much after that. He started working as a handyman again for a wealthy family. My mother worked at a laundry well into her seventies.

My earliest memories are of standing on the corner of the little town square in Hodgenville with my hat on the ground singing for pennies. I used to climb up on the statue of Abraham Lincoln in the square and sit on his lap. I remember that President Roosevelt came to town on a pilgrimage to Lincoln's birthplace. I stood on the steps of the theater and watched him go by. I ran all over that town. My parents were working so I didn't have a lot of supervision.

My uncle had a farm outside of town and I spent a lot of time out there. He lived near the Lincoln Birthplace Memorial and I remember frequently running up and down all those steps. I used to cross the creek by walking on the dam.

We lived in several places including over a grocery store in town. When I was seven, we moved to Louisville. It was right after my oldest sister Evelyn died. She had just been married a few months when she died of a ruptured appendix. That was in 1937 right after the historic flood devasted Louisville. My future wife, Pat, and her family were moving out of Louisville to LaGrange because of the flood while my family was moving in.

In Louisville, we lived on a street that was unpaved and covered in cinders. I used to come home with my bare feet just black. I was a typical boy, fearless and thoughtless.

I was walking home and stepped on a two-by-four with a nail in it. I walked all the way home with that board nailed to my foot. Another time I was reading against a telephone pole and my friend was throwing darts at the pole over my head. I stood up and got a dart through my check. I got shot with a BB gun by my friend. Once my friend and I accidently set a vacant lot on fire. Then we called the fire department and were commended for our quick thinking. We never did tell anyone that we started the fire.

I was very inventive. I made bows and arrows out of umbrella staves. I became quite good at archery until the police put a stop to it because they thought I'd accidently hurt someone. I received an aviator's cap for my birthday and used to use an umbrella and jump off the roof to "parachute out of my plane." My sister, Lil, wasn't too happy that I broke her umbrella. It's a wonder I didn't break something on me.

Once a group of us boys decided to take a whole bunch of root beer and pour it into beer bottles and keep it out in a closet in someone's garage, so we'd have it whenever we were thirsty. It got very hot one day and they all exploded.

We had a cat named Whoopy Cat who used to always fight with our dog, Scrappy. Once Whoopy Cat jumped off the roof onto the back of a boy who was chasing me. I guess he was protecting me.

I played quite a bit of sand lot baseball and football. I broke a rib playing football at the park when five boys tackled me. I could hardly breath with them all on top of me. I passed out. They rolled me over and when I woke up two policemen were standing over me. One was my brother, Paul. He was on the police force for several years. He scolded me and told me to stop playing. I wrapped up my ribs and never told my mother. It's a wonder I survived to adulthood, but I enjoyed my childhood.

Once I got a bicycle, the whole town of Louisville became my backyard. I would ride all over town. I remember going to Churchill Downs and seeing Citation win the Kentucky Derby.

Another time, several boys and I snuck in to the racetrack. We met a man who was a little drunk. He said if we picked a horse for him, we'd split the winnings. We picked a horse that was forty or fifty to one so we could make a fortune. The horse won, but right as we went to collect our winnings, the board flashed that the horse was disqualified for bumping another horse. Our dreams of riches were dashed. That was my last foray into gambling.

I enjoyed watching the western serials that would come on before the movies. The local theater had a promotion where two people could get in for the price of one. I used to walk in with single folks pretending I was with them so I could get in for free and catch every episode. I still love westerns. In my teens, I finally got a job as an usher at a theater so I could legitimately see the movies.

I had to walk about twenty blocks to the elementary school in Parkland. My fourth-grade teacher liked me so much she kept me an extra semester. Maybe it was because she used to make me stand in the coat closet. I would climb out the window, shimmy down the drainpipe and go home.

We went to church in Parkland as well. At one point we lived right next door to my junior high school, and I was still late many times.

I didn't like school. I was small and couldn't compete with some of the other boys. I think that was part of the reason I didn't like school. I graduated from Manuel High School, which was an all-boys school. It went co-ed the year after I graduated. We used to get into fights with the boys from Male High School which was the wealthier school.

I was too small for football and basketball, so I ran track in high school. In the summer I would participate in city track events and was city champion in the hundred-yard dash one year. I ran on a Junior Olympic team in Cleveland. I rode up there on the bus with another boy from Louisville. I didn't win, but it was my first trip out of state. I had the chance to go to the high school state championship meet, but I got sick and couldn't compete.

As I mentioned, I wasn't a good student and graduated in the bottom fourth of my class. When I got my diploma and walked out the door, I told myself it was the last time I'd ever be in a school. I wasn't very motivated academically. The only reason I had even graduated was because I didn't want to disappoint my mother.

My two brothers, Herman and Paul, were lawyers. Paul became a judge. James, or Bud as we called him, was a school teacher for thirty years. I always felt like the black sheep of the family because I didn't know what I wanted to do with my life.

I didn't have much encouragement to go to college, particularly from my older brothers. Because of the age difference, we didn't have a very close relationship. They were grown, married and out of the house when I was in my teens.

All three of my brothers served in World War II. Paul and Herman were in the Navy. Bud tried for months to join the Navy, but they wouldn't accept him for some physical reason. Eventually, he joined the merchant marines. Ironically, after the war he went to college and had just graduated as a teacher, when they drafted him into the Army and sent him to Italy. He wasn't happy about that. Keeping with the family tradition, I joined the Naval Reserves when I graduated from high school. I'll talk more about that later.

I wasn't lazy. I had a lot of jobs. I had a paper route when I was twelve. I worked with a man on a vegetable wagon. I worked at the drug store and at a broom factory. I didn't last long at the broom factory. I was running one of their machines at sixteen and I was supposed to be eighteen. The labor inspector caught me running the machine and the company got fined. I worked at a paint factory and once had to empty a whole boxcar full of paint cans by myself. I worked with my uncle doing electrical work for the school system. I worked for a man who made laundry equipment. I finally got a job at General Electric. I was making cooktops for electric stoves. That was the best paying job I had up until then. I had to leave it to go to college.

In my early twenties I had a health scare. I was at work and my foot was hurting. By the time I got off work it was so swollen I could hardly walk. The next morning, I couldn't set my foot on the floor. My brother took me to the emergency room where it was determined I had blood poisoning. I was in the hospital for ten days, mostly semi-conscious. I remember a nurse helping me, but then she was gone. I asked about her and they said when I was delirious, I had kicked her in the jaw. I felt so bad about that.

At one point I remember a couple of doctors talking in the corner of the room. When I was finally feeling better, I asked one doctor what they had been discussing. I said I had been afraid they were talking about amputating my leg. He said, that's what they had been discussing. Even then, God was protecting me because He had plans for me even though I wasn't walking with Him.

Chapter Two

Turning Point

When I was twenty-two, I went to a revival. I had been a member of the church for years. I joined and was baptized when I was nine. My mother was a very devout Christian and made sure I went to church. I had enough church in me to not be too bad, but too much of the world in me to enjoy serving in the church. I was hanging out in night clubs trying to find some inner satisfaction. Inside I was miserable and had no goals for my life.

I went to the revival feeling depressed and aimless. God spoke to me at that meeting. I ended up asking the Lord into my heart and committing my life to Him. That's the first time I said "Yes" to God. That's why I chose that title for this book. My life truly began that evening as I began my journey with God.

It wasn't too long before I felt He wanted me to go into some sort of ministry. I didn't know what kind of ministry exactly, but in 1953 I entered Georgetown College, a small Southern Baptist College near Lexington, Kentucky. Like I said, I hadn't been a good student and didn't know if I would even be accepted into college. They put me on academic probation and only let me in because I wanted to be a minister. It helped that the college President, Dr. Edelman, was my former pastor from Louisville.

As I mentioned before, I always felt inferior to my brothers. They always seemed to see me as the little brother who wouldn't amount to much. My brother, Herman, told me when I enrolled in college that I was wasting my time and money and would never graduate.

Pat, the girl I was dating was a devout Christian. She had graduated from Georgetown herself and had one year in the seminary. She wanted to be a missionary. One night we were sitting on the porch and I was lamenting that I wasn't capable of being a minister. I didn't have the qualifications or the education, but I felt this tugging from God. "So, you're saying the Lord was mistaken when He called you because you aren't capable?" she asked. That struck a chord. I decided that if He helped me I could do it. Ultimately, I ended up with a bachelor's degree and two master's degrees. Not bad for a man who disliked school.

I was almost twenty-four when I started college. The other students in the dorm called me the "old man". Dr. Edelman took me under his wing, and he would bring me home on the weekends so I could work and see my family and Pat. He took me with him to several revivals and I learned a lot about preaching from him.

Parkland Baptist Church ordained me into the ministry while I was at Georgetown. Dr. Edelman was on my ordination board. He also gave me my diploma when I graduated from college. He left Georgetown to head the Baptist Seminary in New Orleans and urged me to study there, but I wanted to stay in Louisville and go to Southern Seminary.

Chapter Three

Pat

I n 1952, I started dating a girl named Patricia Bell. Mutual friends set us up on a blind date. We went to Clifty Falls State Park across the river in Indiana. We always laughed that you better be careful about going out on blind dates. You never know what might happen.

When I went on one of my Navy deployments to the Bahamas, I sent her back a postcard with a bathing beauty on the beach. She didn't appreciate that, but she kept seeing me.

I went off to college and we continued dating. In my junior year, we decided we should get married. It was a difficult decision for her. She felt called to be a missionary. One of the professors assured her that being a pastor's wife was also a special calling.

My mother was very proud that I was going to be a minister. She was talking to her friends and mentioned that I was going to marry a girl from LaGrange. "Won't that be a problem for your son, since he is going to be a minister?" she asked. "What do you mean," my mother replied. "Well she's from LaGrange, won't that be a problem?" My mother finally realized what she meant. LaGrange was the location of a large women's reformatory. My mother had to reassure her that there was an actual town there as well and that Pat wasn't from the reformatory.

Dr. Edelman thought I should wait until I finished school before I got married, but I told him we were already twenty-five and I didn't think Pat would want to wait for six more years.

We got married in August of 1955 as I was starting into my third year of college. Her father loaned us his car for our honeymoon because he didn't think mine would make it to Kentucky Lake. Ironically, his car broke down and we never made it to the lake. It was years later when we finally made it to the lake for a few days.

In Genesis 2:18 *"The Lord God said, 'It is not good for the man to be alone. I will make a helper suitable for him.'"* I take that Scripture seriously because he gave me the helpmate who was perfect for me. He gave me someone who would be my companion for sixty-two years. She was a helpful, patient, kind and loving person. She was always willing to pack up and move to go where the Lord was sending me. She was an asset in my ministry. All my congregations loved her, too.

We moved into the tiny married quarters at Georgetown. Pat worked in the treasurer's office. My roommate Bob Campbell got married a few weeks after us. He and his wife Renie moved next door. Jack Brown and his wife Jean rounded out our little group at the married housing units.

Times were tough. I went from making $500 a month working at GE to making only $50 a month. Pat was wonderful at stretching every dollar. God always provided. It seemed like when we were down to our last dime, a gift would arrive in the mail from someone that would tide us over.

One semester I needed $120 to pay my spring tuition. I was going to have to stay in Georgetown and work at Sears in Lexington for two weeks which meant that Pat and I couldn't go see our families at Christmas. I was out and saw a help wanted sign. They were looking for a vacuum cleaner salesman. I went in and asked what I'd earn for each vacuum I sold. The man told me I'd earn $20 a piece. I said I'd take six. I took them over to Georgetown and sold them all that day to some of the professors. I made the money for my tuition and we were able to go home for Christmas.

I finished my undergraduate degree a semester early. I think I graduated in the middle of the class, but the Lord had helped me through. I was ready for the next chapter as I was accepted into Southern Baptist Theological Seminary.

Chapter Four

Early Ministry

I was beginning to understand what the Lord wanted me to do, but I didn't yet see the whole picture. College and seminary were the first steps, but I didn't know what else He wanted. I received a telephone call from a church who wanted me to be their pastor. I went to Northern Kentucky to pastor them for two years while I was in college. I became convinced that the Lord wanted me to be a pastor. Things began falling into place.

The first Sunday I preached there, I looked around and there were thirteen people. I had a Sunday school class in my home church in Louisville that was larger than this congregation. It was ok, though, because I knew it was where the Lord wanted me.

They had a cemetery by the church which they kept up, but they let the weeds grow up around the church. I told them we needed to cut the grass because the church looked abandoned. We had thirty-five people coming regularly after that.

There was a woman who was attending, but she wasn't a member. She had been attending for forty years. I asked her why she didn't move her membership and she said she thought she might go back to her old church someday. I told her she had moved all her furniture here. She needed to move her membership, too.

Her husband wasn't a Christian and didn't attend church. Numerous pastors had pestered him about it, but I decided not to say anything to him about it. I had dinner with them one Sunday and he started arguing that he was as good as all those people in that church. I told him that he was probably correct. However, being good wasn't what saved people. It was the grace of God, through faith that saved people. After that Sunday, she came forward and moved her membership and he came right down the aisle after her to accept Christ.

I baptized him in the creek in November. I baptized a nine-year-old girl and a seventy-three-year-old man. There were nine people baptized all together. I was glad when I got a church with a baptistry, and I didn't have to use a freezing cold creek anymore. This experience was another validation of God's calling.

I learned a valuable lesson about children and what they hear and remember. I had taught a children's class and told them about an Olympic runner who refused to run on Sunday because it was the Lord's Day. Months later, I went to the deacons and told them I needed a Sunday off because my wife's family was having a reunion. People were coming from all over including Germany. I didn't realize that one of the nine-year-old boys from that class heard my request. He said, "Preacher, didn't you tell us about that runner who wouldn't run on Sundays? Why don't you tell them you can't go to the picnic on a Sunday?" I felt about an inch tall.

As a pastor, you hear all kinds of excuses as to why people won't come to church. A man told me he didn't like going to the church because the people there weren't very friendly. He said maybe it was a "northern thing". (The church was in Northern Kentucky.). I told him I agreed that the church wasn't very friendly. However, since he and I were friendly "southerners," it was our job to show them how to be friendlier. I asked him to help me do that. He accepted the challenge and returned to church

One Sunday morning, I was preaching and saw a mouse over to the side. I kept preaching but tried to keep my eye on him. I was afraid he was going to come over and sure enough he did. He came and sat on my shoe. I was afraid to move because I thought he might run up my leg. I finally wiggled my foot and he ran off. After church, Pat asked me why I kept jumping around and I told her there had been a mouse on my foot.

I committed to be the best pastor I could be and to get the education I needed to be the best servant of the Lord. My marriage, having a church and having a purpose helped me feel better about myself as well. As I mentioned before, I had never had a purpose or a goal and always felt inferior and aimless. Saying "yes" to God gave my new life direction.

One day, Bob, Jack and I were sitting around drinking coffee and talking about our life goals. I said I wanted to be an Army chaplain and hoped the Lord would let me do that. Bob and Jack both said that was their goal as well. It was interesting that all of us accomplished our goal. Jack enlisted in 1961 during the Berlin Crisis, I enlisted in 1963 and Bob in 1964. We all were chaplains. Bob and I retired as colonels and Jack retired as a lieutenant colonel. We remained friends as we went through Southern Seminary together, as we served in the Army and even to this day.

In addition to the small salary I was earning as a pastor, I needed to earn additional money to pay for seminary. I graduated from college a semester early to try and save up money for seminary in the fall. I had worked at Sears for two weeks at Christmas a couple years in a row while I was in college.

I first went to the state employment office to get a job and they gave me an aptitude test. It showed I should be an engineer. I told them that I was going to be a minister, but they insisted I should be an engineer.

I next went to Sears to see if they had an opening. The human resources clerk said they didn't have anything. The supervisor heard me talking and came out. She called me by name because she remembered me from when I worked there part-time at Christmas. She told me to report to work Monday and they would have a job for me. I was able to work there all through seminary.

I still had the church in Northern Kentucky, but it was a long drive from seminary. I wanted to find a church closer to Louisville. Between going to school, working at Sears and driving hundreds of miles on the weekend to the church near Georgetown, I wasn't spending much time with Pat or committing the time I needed for my school work. I didn't feel like I was giving my best to any area of my life.

One day when I was working at Sears, five people came in all dressed up. They looked like a pulpit committee. They asked if I knew a certain man and if I could go get him. I went to find him and told him I thought a pulpit committee was downstairs asking about him. He said he just accepted a call to a church last week and asked me to tell them he wasn't interested. I relayed the message and out of the blue they asked if I was a minister. I confirmed that I was in school studying to be a minister. They asked me to come talk to them. I met with them and they called me to that church. I stayed for four years. God granted my prayer to find a church closer to school.

A year later, I asked the chairman of the committee why they had gone to Sears to find a minister. He said he had been a farmer for years and knew that Sears had everything you wanted and if they didn't, you could order it. That was another way that God showed me he was guiding me on my journey.

I used to visit families in that community. One family had five girls, but none of them came to church. The parents thought church was just for children. I asked if it would be okay if I came by and picked up the two older children and took them to Bible School. They said ok. The next year I brought three of the children. The third year all five were old enough and came to Bible School. The fourth year, the mother began attending church and a few months before I left the father came.

It's easy to get impatient and want to rush God's work. It took four years to get all seven members of that family in church, but I was doing the job God asked me to do. I was going out and telling people about Him and He was working in their hearts in His own time.

There was a fifteen-year old boy at the church who always wanted me to go hunting with him. I kept refusing. One day I was at his home for dinner. He was excited to show me the new .22 rifle he had just received for his birthday. He asked me to go hunting with him again, and again I said no. He finally decided that I didn't want to go hunting because as a minister I didn't know how to shoot a rifle. When he told me that I asked if I could see his rifle. I looked out across the field and saw a fence post with a grasshopper on it. I told him to watch the post. I shot the rifle. He ran out to the post, convinced I'd missed my shot. Then he looked on the ground and saw the two halves of the grasshopper. He didn't ask me to go hunting again.

After about a year, one of the deacons came to me and told me things just weren't working out and all the deacons agreed that I needed to leave. I was upset because I thought things had been going well. It made me question my decision to go into the ministry.

I turned in my resignation that Sunday and got up and said I understood from the deacon that they all wanted me to leave. The next week I went to preach what I thought was my last sermon. Afterwards the moderator got up and said they held a business meeting the night before and voted to have me stay. The deacon got up and said, "I told them if you are staying, I am leaving." He did leave, but I stayed for another three years.

I found out later that the boy with the hunting rifle and his teenage sister planned to go to the business meeting. They found out their parents didn't plan to attend because they didn't want to upset that deacon. The teens said they were going to go and vote to keep the pastor. I think they shamed their parents into going as well.

Pat, as always, was a big help and without her I wouldn't have made it through seminary. She typed all my papers and worked at GE to help support us while I was in school. I knew I was on the right track and that I was doing what God wanted. I graduated from the seminary and continued pastoring.

My daughter, Connie, was born right before my graduation ceremony. My son, Donald Ray, was born eighteen months later.

After I graduated from the seminary, my first church was at New Providence, a small, rural American Baptist church outside of Scottsburg, Indiana, about thirty miles north of Louisville. A group of men came down from the church to help us move. They did a good job.

Pat was pregnant at the time. She had suffered several miscarriages and was supposed to take it easy. Her mother, Gypsie, came to help with the move and was directing the movers, telling them what to do. Pat was giving her mother directions, too. One of the deacons got home and was talking to his wife. She asked what he thought about the new pastor and his wife. He said that they seemed nice, but that the preacher's wife was lazy as can be. She just sat there in the chair and told her mother what to do. She didn't do anything to help. His wife replied that Pat was expecting and had some health problems, which was why she wasn't helping.

A few months later we had dinner with them. I happened to say something about my wife being as lazy as can be. He was embarrassed that we had heard about what he said, but it became a joke between us.

New Providence has always been a special church for us.

Forty-five years later I went back to New Providence and did an interim for eighteen months and it was just like coming home. When Pat passed away, several people came up from New Providence for the funeral.

Connie was the first baby living in their parsonage. Donald was born two years later. One of the men built a sandbox for the children. There were several teenage girls in the church who always took care of the children. Pat directed the choir and I was preaching. As soon as we walked in the church door someone would grab them and take care of them throughout the service. We didn't have to buy anything for the children for two years because someone was always giving us clothes and toys.

There was a man who used to walk all over town and would walk by the house often. One day I was out in the yard and we started chatting. I happened to mention that we had been planning a trip to Florida but didn't have the money to go. He gave me some advice that I never forgot. He said he used to work for the railroad. He and his wife never went anywhere. When they retired, they planned to travel the world. Then they planned to come back and use his railroad pass to travel the United States. A few months before he retired, she died. "Take your wife to Florida," he told me. "Don't wait to travel."

We stayed at New Providence for three years and I became oriented into the American Baptist Convention. I worked frequently with the Area Minister to learn about the Convention and the various churches.

I drew up some plans and had talked to a contractor about the cost to build an educational building. The church only had a small basement and it was hard for the older people to get down the stairs to the classrooms and restrooms. There was some resistance to the idea of building the addition. They didn't think they had the money. The year after I left, they finally got it built. They invited me to the groundbreaking and had me turn over the first shovel of dirt.

The parsonage was across the street and it was very small. It was fine for us because both the children were small. It had a coal furnace and had a problem with hard water. I told my wife, if a minister with older children came to serve here, this place would be too small for them. Forty-five years later when I went down to do an interim pastorate, they still hadn't expanded the parsonage. They had a picture on the wall that showed the plans for expanding the parsonage. The plans were four years old already and they hadn't done anything. Before I left as an interim pastor, they finally added an extension to almost double its size.

When I felt God wanted me to leave New Providence, I wasn't sure where exactly He wanted me to go. I got a call from a church in Superior, Wisconsin. Pat and I went up and visited, but it seemed so far away, and it would be very cold in the winter. I struggled with the decision because they had a unanimous vote for me to come. I prayed about it and felt that the Lord didn't want me to go up there.

A church nearby in Orleans called me. It was a small town with about two thousand people, but the church was larger. I felt the Lord was leading me there. They had a beautiful parsonage that was about twice the size of the one in Scottsburg.

When we discussed coming over, they talked about how much bigger they were than New Providence and the opportunities their church could provide. They wanted to pay me the same salary, but I told them there would be more work and my children were growing. They finally agreed to a salary increase.

Again, the church needed additional space and they had plans to expand their current building. They had a yard between the church and the parsonage they wanted to use for the expansion. I didn't think that would work. The previous pastor had supported using the old building with an add-on. I kept thinking about it for three months.

I had a friend, who was a painter, draw up what the church would look like using the plans they were considering. I put it up on the wall for the congregation to see. After a few weeks at a business meeting I asked them if that was the direction they wanted to go. They said that plan had been the old pastor's plan and they agreed it wasn't a good idea to add on to a hundred-year-old building. They decided to build a whole new building.

While I was there, they got their finances in order. The income of the church doubled. They voted a budget, they voted to pay into my retirement and to provide insurance for me. That helped me, but it also put them in good shape to attract future pastors. After the business meeting, one of the deacons came up and said there had been four people who voted against the salary increase I asked for when I first came. It was him, his wife, his father and his mother. They thought I was in it for the money. Now that they had worked with me the last few months, they realized I was only interested in improving the church. This time they supported the benefits package and the raise.

The day after the vote, I received a phone call saying that I was being called up to active duty. I had been in the Navy and then the Army Reserves for about twelve years now. I was to report in January to school for active duty. I talked to the denomination and they confirmed that they had an opening and they wanted me to fill it.

When I told the church I had to leave, they were disappointed. We had been accomplishing a lot and I felt we were moving in the direction God wanted. I baptized a father and son right before I left. I was only there fifteen months, but it was a good fifteen months.

My philosophy as a pastor was that all these churches were God's. I always let every church know that while I might make mistakes, I never would do anything to hurt the church. I believe that with God's help, I left every church in better shape than when I came.

Chapter Five

Military Service

Back in the day, you had to serve eight years in the military. I was too young for World War II, but I joined the Naval Reserves out of high school. I served during the Korean War even though I was never called up to go to Korea. I served nine years in the Navy which met my eight years of mandatory service. I started as a Seaman Recruit and was a gunner's mate.

I did my training at Great Lakes Naval Base. I went up on the bus with another boy from Louisville. There were many boys there from Pennsylvania and Detroit. One night the boy from Louisville and I were talking. Everyone else was very quiet. I finally turned to the others and asked why they were so quiet. The boy from Detroit said, "We's guys like to hear you's guys say ya'll".

As I mentioned before, I was an excellent shot. I had used a .22 a lot when I was growing up. At Great Lakes, I came in second in the sharpshooting competition. I lost to a boy who was a trapper in the Louisiana bayous. I was able to travel quite a bit during my two-week deployments with the Navy each year. I had hardly been out of Kentucky until I joined the Navy, but my time in the Navy helped foster my love of travel.

Once our unit was sent to Transylvania College in Kentucky to help protect President Eisenhower when he came to give a speech. Mostly, we made a lot of training runs up and down the Ohio River.

In the Navy I learned that if you talk to people when you travel, you will find the world is a small place. There is always someone who knows someone you know. I went to sea duty and I was not with anyone else from home. I boarded the ship in Norfolk to go to the Caribbean for training. I thought surely, I wouldn't know anyone there. I was down in the engine room one evening talking to a fellow seaman. He asked me where I was from. I told him I was in school in Kentucky. He asked me the name of the school. I told him it was a small school. "I'm sure you haven't heard of it." He asked the name and I told him Georgetown. It turned out he had a brother there who roomed two doors down from me in the dorm.

On another trip back from the Caribbean, a huge storm came up and the ship was rocking badly. Many of the crew were seasick. The cook couldn't prepare hot meals for four days. Water was coming over the sides. I wasn't the only one praying for safety that day.

When I started thinking about becoming a chaplain, I wanted to go into the Army. The Vietnam War was heating up. Since I missed World War II and Korea, I felt I owed Uncle Sam some combat time. I also felt called to minister to the young soldiers who were being drafted into service.

To be a chaplain, you had to be endorsed by your denomination. I applied through the Southern Baptist denomination, but they kept telling me they didn't have any slots. I kept getting older. The age cap was thirty-three for joining and I was thirty-one already.

When I went to the church in Scottsburg, it was an American Baptist Church. I stayed there three years. After three years of serving in an American Baptist Church, I would be eligible to be recommended by the American Baptist denomination as a chaplain. They had openings for chaplains. God knew I needed to change to the American Baptist Church if I was going to enter the Army and He sent me to New Providence

The Executive Minister in Indianapolis wrote a letter to the mission board asking them to waive the three-year requirement to two-years so I wouldn't age out. The mission board approved the request, but only allowed me to enter the Reserves. They would not approve me for active duty until I completed that third year.

I still needed the Army to approve my commission. There was a man in the church in New Providence who was an officer in the Army reserves. He came up to me and said he'd heard I wanted to be a chaplain. I told him I did, but they didn't have any openings and my age was catching up with me. He asked if I had thought about joining the reserves. He said he had a unit in Jeffersonville, Indiana with an opening for a chaplain. It turns out the commander of the unit was my principal from junior high school. Despite that, he offered me a position and I put in the paper work for a commission.

I was down to nine months before I reached the age cap when I put in the request. It got hung up somewhere in Michigan, so I called the chaplain up there and he said he'd find it and pass it on through. It was signed three months before my 33rd birthday.

As a Chaplain, I was commissioned by the denomination as a missionary. I always felt that made Pat the missionary she wanted to be.

I was commissioned as a first lieutenant. I served in the reserve unit for three years. I met many young soldiers who needed spiritual guidance. Working with them reaffirmed my conviction that God was calling me to minister to them.

When I received the call up to active duty, I left Pat and the children in LaGrange, Kentucky near her family while I went to Ft. Hamilton, New York for Chaplain's School. After school I was posted to Ft. Leonard Wood, Missouri. It was a training base for soldiers. It was exactly what I wanted.

The brigade there was too large, so they decided to split it into two brigades. I was very surprised when my commander called and said he was going over to the new brigade and wanted me to go with him. I was very honored that he asked. I was only three months out of school.

A brigade normally has three chaplains, usually a major and two captains. I was just a lieutenant and ended up as the Brigade Chaplain by myself. It was a year before they finally assigned the brigade more help. My assistant, (we were supposed to have three), and I were responsible for thirty-five hundred soldiers.

We all knew most of the soldiers were training to go to Vietnam. Most were draftees and they needed counseling and spiritual guidance.

We would get two new companies of soldiers every week -- about five hundred soldiers. They would stay for eight weeks of training. They would march the new soldiers over to the chapel so they would know where it was. I would talk to them about the services the chaplain provided. The former chaplains would then have them marched in for the service. I put a stop to that. I told them they were welcome to stay for the service, but they weren't obligated. I didn't feel the Lord wanted me to coerce people into church because of my rank. We still always packed out the services.

In addition to ministering, I also had to rebuild and fix up the chapel which had been vacant for several years. The post commander wanted to beautify the post by planting flowers and landscaping. His wife was enthusiastically behind that project. She came to my chapel and asked me what I thought of this initiative and if I thought the soldiers appreciated it. I told her they appreciated the effort. Then I said, "Ma'am, it's a shame that the chapel, which is right by the front gate and two buildings from headquarters. is rundown and needs painting. I wish it looked decent." I wasn't sure if I was doing the right thing by saying this to her.

On Monday morning the general was on my doorstep. He said, "This chapel is rundown and needs painting and fixing." I told him I'd put in six work orders and they kept telling me there was no money to fill them. He told me to send them in again and sure enough, the painters and maintenance showed up right away to fix everything up. The general's wife was even picking out drapes.

We used to have weekly staff meetings. The practice was that if you were late, you bought drinks for everyone after the meeting. I would go with them to the officer's club afterwards to socialize even though I didn't drink. One day I was late. We arrived at the club and the bartender asked who would be buying the drinks. The executive officer told him the chaplain would. Without me saying anything, the colonel spoke up and told him that the chaplain didn't buy drinks. The executive officer protested that I had been late. The colonel told him that if the chaplain was late, he had a good reason.

That executive officer was going to be my rater and I was on his bad side after that incident. When it came time for evaluations, the colonel took my evaluation away from him and said that the general would be my rater. I appreciated the colonel looking out for me because I would have received a bad evaluation which would have gone on my record and impacted my promotion.

The colonel helped me in another important way. He reviewed my records and saw my reserve time. He realized that I was eligible for promotion, so he had the paperwork submitted to the promotion board. He called Pat and I into his office one Saturday morning. I thought I was in trouble for something. Instead he promoted me to Captain. He said I should have been promoted sixteen months ago. Almost a year later I received backpay for the sixteen months which was a big help financially.

I worked hard and spent a lot of time with the soldiers. I went out in the field with them. I wanted to be a good chaplain. Someone asked me what I could do when I only had a soldier for eight weeks. I said my goal was to give them a good experience with a chaplain so that when they got to their new unit they would trust and respect their chaplain.

When I went to Vietnam, I was at an aid station visiting some wounded soldiers in my unit. A soldier called out to me by name. I knew he wasn't one of my people from my unit. I asked how he knew my name. He said eight months ago I was his chaplain at Ft. Leonard Wood. I told him I was surprised he remembered my name. He said, "I was there for your last sermon at the fort and I even remember what you preached about." That reaffirmed that people were listening and that I was being the example God wanted me to be.

I enjoyed Ft. Leonard Wood. As I mentioned, I had a lot of support from the commanding officers at that post. The colonel used to hand out bulletins at the service. When I left, I was replaced by a major and two captains. I'm still in touch with that assistant. He was a very good, young soldier and helped me so much in that first assignment.

Chapter Six

Vietnam

I joined the Army to go to Vietnam. I got my wish in 1966. I took my family to the "waiting-wives location" which had been set up at Schilling Air Base in Kansas. Pat decided she'd rather go there than go back to her family in Kentucky. The children were three and five. I think it did make it easier for her and the children. All the "daddies" were overseas. The women were all without their husbands and dealing with being responsible for the family. It created a built-in support system for Pat.

I left for Vietnam the day after Christmas in 1966. It was an interesting trip. I left about 10 a.m. with a warrant officer. He wasn't very knowledgeable about chaplains. We missed the plane in Wichita and had to go back to Kansas City to catch another flight. The place was packed with soldiers going back to duty after Christmas and I didn't think there was any way we'd get a flight, but we were number one and two and made the flight. We made it to California and got bumped off our connection there. The pilot put in a good word for us and got us on the first plane out. It arrived earlier than our original connection. We flew into Honolulu. We were supposed to have an hour layover.

The warrant officer said "I've never been to Hawaii and would love to go to Waikiki. Is there anything you can do?" I said I'd see what I could do. They told us to go get breakfast which we did. Then they told us to go get a hotel because they needed a part and we had to spend the night. The warrant officer and I were able to go down to the beach and enjoy Hawaii for an evening. We arrived in Vietnam finally. I was going north, he was going south. The warrant officer stopped me and said "We'll probably go back around the same time next year. Do you think we could go to Japan?" I laughed.

I spent a night in Saigon waiting for transportation to my unit up north. I watched *Gunsmoke* on the TV in the restaurant. I went to bed with the mosquito netting over me. In the middle of the night, I felt something going across my chest. I woke up and looked around and didn't see anything. The next thing I felt were my dog tags rattling and I knew something was in there with me. I scrambled out one end while something went out the other. I never knew what it was, but the country had huge rats. That was my introduction to Vietnam.

I arrived at my unit near Tuy Hòa. I was assigned to a combat engineer battalion. We were responsible for keeping the main highway, QL1, open and mine-free. Their chaplain had been gone almost a month before I arrived. Everybody thought I'd be like the other chaplain, which apparently wasn't a good thing. I let it be known that I was me and would do things differently, but that I'd come to serve them the best way I knew how.

I hadn't been there very long and was in the mess hall drinking coffee. A sergeant came in and asked me why we had a chaplain for an engineering outfit. He claimed they didn't need one. I told him that if you looked at your unit requirements, it says that a combat engineer battalion has one chaplain and one assistant. I was there to fill that slot per regulation.

A month later, I experienced my first casualties. We had a memorial service for five young men who had been killed. It was sad to have this funeral, but I knew I'd need to get used to it. The same sergeant came up and told me he went to the service and now knew why they needed a chaplain.

The soldiers had a Constitutional right to religious services while they were in a combat zone and I was committed to be available to them wherever they were. That was my goal.

I learned at Ft. Leonard Wood that you deal with the officers and the NCOs, but you always start at the bottom of the chain with your requests. I was always careful not to go over someone's head unless I needed something for the troops.

It bothered me that they had put up showers for the troops, but there was no privacy. There were several Vietnamese women working in the camp cleaning and cooking who would walk by those showers. I complained that the soldiers deserved to have some privacy and got them to put up some canvas around the showers.

Once I was down at Cam Ranh Bay which was the main headquarters. It was a beautiful place and used a lot for rest and relaxation (R&R) for the soldiers. I was there on leave and overheard one of the sergeants being rude to another soldier who was there on R&R. I went up to him and said, "You mustn't like your job." "What do you mean he asked?" I replied, "Your job is to help facilitate off-time for these troops. If you're not happy with your job, I can send you up north where he is assigned." (That was an area of heavy fighting). "Oh, no," he said, "don't do that." I told him I never wanted to hear him being rude to those boys again.

The engineers were a great unit. They worked hard and played hard, but they were very dedicated to doing their job. I was proud to be a member of the 39th Combat Engineer Battalion.

We had seven companies that I served. I tried to keep track of the troops in my unit. I had nineteen hundred soldiers scattered over almost a hundred miles. I was conducting thirty services a month and was on the road six days a week. I even covered a marine unit when the Navy moved to the north and their chaplain moved north as well. The marines were left behind and appreciated my coming to minister to them. They'd always have cake or pie or coffee for me when I'd land.

I was on the road a lot or in a helicopter going to the various companies to hold services. Every time you went out you had to worry about snipers and mines, but my job was to go out and serve, not stay back at camp.

Like I said, we were tasked with keeping the road open. Once, I went up to the end of the line to serve some of the engineers. When I got back to camp, I got chewed out for going up there when the road wasn't officially open.

We were often out ahead of the other units. I remember we had been working on a road for three months. The 101st Airborne moved into the area. They put up a sign that read "Sleep well. You're protected by the 101st Airborne." My folks weren't very happy about that. We'd been there protecting ourselves just fine for all those months.

Attendance was always good at the services. Only once did the units miss out on having a weekly service. I was proud of that. They may not have attended every service, but I did my job giving them the opportunity to worship.

Although all the chaplains I worked with were doing a good job, I heard all sorts of stories about chaplains sitting in their office and not doing their job. I was determined not to be one of them.

There was a young man who hung around the chapel often. He wanted to be my assistant, but I already had one. I was afraid he'd get in trouble for hanging out in the chapel and not doing his work. The commander noticed. I advised the commander to send him out to one of the other companies away from headquarters. The soldier came and told me he was moving out. I told him, he could be good for those troops at his new unit by helping them spiritually. I checked on him later and he was having a Bible study for his comrades. He was serving God more than if he'd been my assistance.

My assistant used to drive me to the various locations so I could hold services. I told my commander that it bothered me that when I went out to a service, I was endangering my assistant and others who often would go to protect me. He said, "Chaplain, your job is to have services. You're doing a good job. It's their job to get you where you're going and to protect you. Everyone has their own responsibilities."

I rode in helicopters a lot. I was like a rabbit's foot and never had trouble bumming a ride. Once, the denomination sent an endorsing agent over to observe me in Saigon. It was mandatory that I meet with him. The commander said he didn't think there was any way I could get down there because of a lack of transportation. The colonel was going to Saigon as well and took a helicopter. I bummed a ride on a different helicopter, met with my agent and had a good visit. (My endorsing agent came every year, wherever I was to make sure I was doing a good job and representing them well). I went to find a ride back to the unit. I found a pilot to give me a ride and I ended up getting back two days earlier than the colonel because he was still waiting for a ride.

The helicopters flew with the doors open. Most of the time there weren't even any seatbelts. You just had to hang on and hope you didn't fall out. One time I was on the outside edge and was taking pictures out the door. The pilot decided to try and scare me by tilting the helicopter. I just looked at him and told him to tilt a little more so I could get my pictures.

Another time I was in a small, bubble helicopter with just me and the pilot. He asked me how well I could throw. I asked why he wanted to know. He said he needed to throw out some smoke bombs. I said I didn't think I could do that. He handed me the stick and made me fly the helicopter for a few minutes while he threw them out.

A lot of scary things happened in Vietnam. I was hitching a ride one time and got on the helicopter. The pilot was trying to get off the ground, but it was so hot and humid he couldn't get any lift. He made me and another fellow get off. He turned it and we got on. He still couldn't get into the air, so we got off again. He turned it facing down a hill and we got on again and he launched off the hill to get lift and we made it up. We would sometimes fly so low you could put your helmet on a water buffalo.

I always prayed for the helicopter pilots and their passengers. When I was on the hospital ship, there were five helicopter pilots with me and among all of them they didn't have more than five weeks in country. They were shot down often and had one of the most dangerous jobs.

One day a boy came to talk to me. He wasn't wearing his helmet and I told him he was out of uniform and I wouldn't talk to him until he had his helmet on. He left and didn't come back. I assumed I'd offended him. The next morning, he came back and thanked me. I asked him why. He said, "Look at this helmet. Last night we were under a mortar attack and if you hadn't made me go put my helmet on, I'd be dead."

I would tell the sergeants when I wanted to have services and tried to keep with the schedule. Some often gave me a hard time and said they were in a combat zone and couldn't carve out time for church services. I would tell them that if the troops had time to eat and sleep, there was time for a service if the soldiers wanted to worship. The commander supported me, though, so they couldn't do more than just complain.

I had two Catholic soldiers who would help me set up for the Protestant church service at one of the units. I asked them why they were willing to help. They said they knew I was trying to get them a priest, but until one arrived, they'd come to my service.

Once a unit had their Protestant chaplain killed. One of the priests asked me to go with him to have services for them. He was telling the troops that he was going to have mass in a few minutes and that I would have a Protestant service at the other end of the camp. A soldier came up and said he wasn't Catholic or Protestant. The priest told him to "go to hell then." The soldier went to the Catholic service. Afterwards, I commented that what he said was harsh. He told me these men were going out on a mission and many wouldn't come back. "I didn't have time to argue with him about religion," he said.

One day General Westmoreland came for an award ceremony and I was able to take some pictures of him. They practically stopped the war for his visit.

A few months later, we moved to a new area. Five units were moving north to a more dangerous area and two were staying behind. I knew about the move, but it wasn't general knowledge. A few days before we left, a soldier came to me complaining about his sergeant. He wanted to transfer to a different company. I knew the company he was in was one of the two remaining in the safer area, so I urged him not to transfer. I thought I had convinced him to stay.

We loaded up most of the camp on LSTs and offloaded on the beach further north near Chu Lai. There were almost a thousand soldiers on that beach, and we took some fire. The first casualty was that soldier I thought I had convinced to stay with his unit.

We remained on the beach until the engineers built the road into Duc Pho. They had to build it across rice paddies. It was about four miles to Duc Pho. After we made it to Duc Pho, the engineers were tasked with building a road to a new airfield.

The marines had built a wooden structure we were using for a chapel. One day I saw a soldier and the lieutenant huddled by the chapel. I went over to see what was going on. They asked if I had a pet snake. I said, no. They said there was a huge cobra inside. Word got around that there was a snake in the chapel which hurt attendance for a while until we caught it.

The cots were uncomfortable because they sagged. It was bothering my back, so I put a board down to provide some support. One night I was trying to sleep and heard this chewing noise. I looked under that board and bunch of mice had made a nest in the wood.

I held services everywhere – in mess halls, under bridges, on beaches, and in huts. Wherever the soldiers were, I would go, too.

Partway through my tour, I had the opportunity to go on seven days R&R. I had the option of going to Singapore, Australia, the Philippines or Hawaii. I chose Hawaii so that Pat could join me, and we could spend some time together. I didn't want to go to the beach since I'd been living on beaches for six months, but we had a nice time.

It was hard leaving her and going back. I was so homesick. It took me about a month to settle back in. I was jumpy thinking that I wasn't going to see her again. That was the only week my troops ever missed a service. I had asked another chaplain to cover for me, but he didn't do it, which upset me.

No place was secure, but you had to just live with that knowledge. I didn't sleep soundly the whole time I was in country. You always had to be alert for mortar attacks at night. When we pitched our tents, we had to dig bunkers to protect ourselves.

A soldier was going to take a big dump truck out to act as guard. He arrived at the work site and a sergeant told him to get off. "You're going home in a month and don't need to be on the road". The sergeant climbed on and acted as shotgun. Another sergeant told the first sergeant to get off because he needed to go that way anyway. He drove just a few yards and hit a mine and lost his legs. I can't explain why things like that happen, but I clung to the knowledge that God was in control.

I remember we were driving to one area. The vehicle in front of us was a courier. The driver was Catholic. He said chaplain, "I just got word they have sniper fire on the road ahead. I wish you'd bless my jeep". Even though that wasn't a Baptist thing, I blessed his jeep. We started down the road and we didn't have any trouble. He thanked me and said he knew we'd be safe because I had blessed his jeep. I was glad to give him some peace of mind.

I went to a unit to have service and talked to the sergeant. I said, "You always get your men to the service, but you never come yourself." He said, "I've got too much to do. When I get home, I'll start going to church." I said, "You know, and I know that we may not get home. You need to get right with God now." I left him there. Two hours later I received a radio message that he had been shot twice in the back by a sniper and was on the hospital ship. He died a few hours later. If there is something you need to do, you need to do it now. God does not promise us tomorrow.

When I left for Vietnam, I had to get things in order. I had to have a will and get my finances in order to support my family in case something happened to me. I had to get insurance and all my affairs settled. I had to prepare myself to die. I learned a spiritual truth that you need to be ready to meet the Lord and then you can live your life without worrying.

Often, we had services with snipers shooting. I heard a story about a chaplain who was having a service and the enemy started firing on them. He was getting ready to have the prayer. He said, "Go in peace, but go in a hurry."

I was at an aid station when a company tried to hold a hill. Almost all the soldiers were lost in the fight. I helped at the aid station as the casualties came in. I tried not to worry my wife by telling her some of the situations I was in, but she saw the news one evening and found out I had been in that area.

In Vietnam, I saw people at their best and at their worst. I saw acts of heroism and courage. Despite the civil rights turmoil going on back in the States, I saw a black sergeant run under heavy fire out into a field to rescue a white soldier who had been shot. He carried him out on his back all the while taking fire.

I sat with a wounded soldier's head in my lap. He had blood all over him and was unable to see. We were waiting on the beach for an evac helicopter to take him to the hospital. He kept asking for his buddies and I couldn't bear to tell him they had all been killed.

The soldiers cared so much for each other. Most of the soldiers I met were honest, good people who did their duty and were just trying to make it through to the end of their tour. The war often seemed senseless, but it was where God had placed me.

I never regretted my time in Vietnam. In some ways, it was the high point of my life because I felt I was the most useful there.

Vietnam was a beautiful country. Flying over the country in helicopters you could see the beauty of the mountains and the fields above the ugliness of the war. I always took my camera with me to photograph the countryside and the people.

The people there were just trying to survive. The children were always smiling even when they had nothing. The Vietnamese people were just like people everywhere. They were mostly farmers who only wanted to plant their rice and feed their families. Our unit would help dig wells for them to provide clean water. The North Vietnamese would often come in at night and destroy them.

There was an airstrip where we would pick up sick children and take them to the hospitals. The Northern Vietnamese would tell the people that we were going to throw their children out of the helicopters. The families were desperate, though, and would take the chance to try to get medical care for their children. It is a shame there's always someone trying to take what little others have.

I boarded a helicopter one Sunday at noon to go and hold some services. My assistant wanted to go with me, but I told him to stay behind and finish up some letters. One of my jobs was to write condolence letters to families. He was upset with me because I wouldn't let him go with me. I woke up eight days later aboard a hospital ship on the way to the Philippines.

I was told the helicopter landed and I conducted services. I needed to go four more miles down the road for the next service. Two soldiers volunteered to take me there. Two Vietnamese set off a two-hundred-pound bomb under our jeep. It blew a hole in the road twenty feet long, eight feet wide and eight feet deep. I was thrown out almost fifty yards into a rice patty into waist-deep mud. If I hadn't landed sitting up, I would have drowned.

God was watching over me, but those two nineteen-year old boys were blown apart. I never learned their names, but they are listed on the wall in Washington, DC. By all rights my name should have been there as well. I can't comprehend it or understand it completely. I tried to find comfort in what that major had told me. It was my job to serve and it was their job to transport and protect me. I was thirty-five-years-old. I vowed that if I wasted my life, it would be a tragedy because it meant those boys gave their life for nothing. God allowed me to survive because he had more work for me to do.

(I caught up with my assistant several years later when he was teaching in California. He recognized my voice right away when I called and thanked me repeatedly for making him stay behind that day. We have kept in touch over the years and I talked with him just a few months ago.)

That ended my tour in Vietnam. My staff Chaplain wrote me a commendation letter which I still cherish. It stated that wherever he went in the units and asked about the chaplain, everyone always knew me by name and by sight and only had good things to say about me. My willingness to go wherever I was needed, even into dangerous situations, led to my being awarded the Bronze Star. I received a Purple Heart as well.

Before I was wounded, our doctor had been pestering me to get a flu shot. I told him I wasn't going to get one because the last one had made me sick. He said you can't leave Vietnam unless you get a flu shot. I was adamant that I wasn't going to get one. I heard later from one of the unit sergeants I saw after I was back in the States that the doctor had said, "I've never had someone go to such extremes to avoid a flu shot."

Don and James 1934

High School Senior Picture 1949

Pop, Don and Mom

Don and Pat, 1954

Don and Pat's Wedding, 1955

Graduation from Georgetown College – Lilian, Aunt Katherine, Don, Thelma and Mom

Baptism in Northern Kentucky

Pat, Don and Connie 1961

Graduation from Seminary

Connie, Don and Donald, Ft. Leonard Wood

Vietnam, 1967

Services on the Beach

Don's Jeep and Tent

Easter Sunrise Services in Vietnam, 1967

Don's office in Vietnam

Wreckage of Don's Jeep

USS Sanctuary

Janes "Bud" came to visit during Don's recovery

Chaplain's Conference in Berchtesgaden and the family in Germany, 1971

Chapel Service

Chaplain Humphrey

Promotion to Colonel

Pastor Don

Preparing a Sermon

Parade at Bunker Hill

Lilian, Bud, Paul, Don and Herman at Don's Retirement

Dan, Pat and their camper

Pat and Don Traveling

Connie, Donald, Pat and Don in Alaska, 2005

Pat, Don and Connie in Australia, 2015

Don's return to Hodgenville, KY 2018

Chapter Seven

Recovery

I was on the hospital ship, the *USS Sanctuary*, for thirty days. They had two hospital ships in the area. I don't remember much about the ship because I was unconscious for about ten days. I had numerous injuries. I broke all the ribs on my left side in multiple places, punctured my ear drums, had damage to my lungs, and broke my arm.

They sent my wife three telegrams. The first said that I was wounded and wasn't expected to live. The second telegram a few days later said I would live, but I would probably have brain damage. The third telegram said I was improving.

When I woke up, I remember seeing a man in white. I reached out to see if he was real. They did a tracheotomy to help me breath. The medical staff gave me excellent care even though one day one of them threatened to put a marble down the hole in my throat if I didn't behave. The *USS Sanctuary* took the most serious casualties and I was one of them. I was in ICU and then in critical care and finally released to the ward. I had two orthopedists and a neurologist working on me.

The ship headed to the Philippines to transport some of the patients back to the U.S. On the way a storm struck. Everyone around me became sick except me and another soldier. Even the navy personnel got seasick. We arrived in the Philippines, but the doctor wouldn't clear me for transport. I had to stay on the ship for ten days while we were in Subic Bay harbor.

It was interesting that while my brother Bud was with the merchant marines during World War II, his ship came to the Philippines. The regular navy wouldn't let the merchant mariners off the ship and made them offload cargo by barge. He stayed out on the ship for ten days in Subic Bay and was never able to go ashore either.

Instead of transporting me from the Philippines, the ship went back to Vietnam. We stayed overnight and they were expecting mortar attacks. I thought that was all I needed. I survive a bomb and instead get killed in a mortar attack. Fortunately, the attack didn't happen, and the ship went on to Japan.

I saw Tokyo looking out the window laying on my back on a stretcher as we travelled to the air base. They thought it would be three weeks before I was transported stateside. Instead, the second day they flew me to Denver.

I did have a chance to call Pat while I was in Japan. The way it worked was the military would pay the charges for the call to a relay station in the U.S., but you had to pay the charge from the relay station to your house. We never received a bill for that call. I found out later that Senator Barry Goldwater paid for it. He was a ham radio operator and would forward the calls for soldiers for free.

I arrived in California and then was transported to Fitzsimmons Military Hospital in Denver. I was wearing a pair of pajamas and a wrist band with my name on it. That's all I had with me. When I arrived, it was three degrees. That was a huge temperature change from Vietnam. I thought I was going to freeze. The altitude made it hard to breathe with my broken ribs. I had received a package from the Red Cross in Japan with some toiletries. I didn't have identification, money, or clothes. What upset me the most was that I had lost my wedding ring.

I spent five months at the hospital in Denver. I was having problems with my hearing. I had physical therapy on my broken arm. It took a long time for everything to heal. My ribs were still hurting after a year. I can't praise those military doctors and nurses enough.

After a few months, I was just healing and didn't need constant medical care. They moved me out of the hospital into quarters. I was still receiving full pay. The Tet Offensive had begun, and we were receiving many new casualties into the hospital. I asked permission to have a ward that I could be responsible for so I could minister to the other patients. They said they had never let a patient do that, but the chaplain agreed to give me a ward to serve. I'm not the type of person to just sit around. That gave me another way to serve the troops.

The hospital chaplain was very good to me. One day, he took me over to the Air Force Academy. I appreciated that gesture from him.

Lying in my room one day, I heard a commotion. A man and woman came in and stood by my bed. It was a young couple I had pastored at New Providence. I'd performed their wedding ceremony before I left for Vietnam and Connie had been their flower girl. He was stationed in Colorado Springs and they had come to check on me. They heard somehow from the church about my injuries. The convention had put out a newsletter with the information that I'd been wounded. It was nice seeing familiar faces.

They visited several times. After several months, they came to take me out on a car tour of Denver. I checked with the doctor to get permission and he said that would be fine, but he told me he had been planning to give me a thirty-day convalescent leave that day. I told him I was sure my friends would understand if I turned down the tour and went home instead.

I had to borrow some clothes from another chaplain to wear home. When I joined the Army, I weighed 167 pounds. After training I was down to 147 pounds. I left the hospital weighing 113 pounds. The clothes were too big, but I appreciated them so much. My possessions still had not arrived from Vietnam.

I met my wife and children at the airport at Schilling Air Force Base. I remember my son saying, "That doesn't look like my Daddy." Then I spoke to him with that trach hole still not fully healed in my throat and he said, "That doesn't sound like my Daddy either." I was so happy to be home after sixteen months.

My son came in one day looking for Pat. He wanted permission to do something. I told him he could do whatever it was. He said, "You mean you can say it's OK." He had been so used to Pat being responsible for everything.

I spent thirty days at home then went back to the hospital. As I mentioned, all the housing at Schilling had been turned over to the wives and children waiting for their husbands serving in Vietnam. It was strange being one of the only men there.

Chapter Eight

More Military Assignments

A few weeks after returning to the hospital in Denver, they released me and reassigned me to Ft. Dix, New Jersey. I kept asking to be assigned to Ft. Lewis in Washington state. My fellow chaplain with the same rank and from the same denomination wanted to go to Ft. Dix. Instead, I went to Ft. Dix and he went to Ft. Lewis. That's the Army.

Ft. Dix was another training facility. I was able to work with the troops again, which I enjoyed. I received a Commendation Medal for my work there.

While I was at Ft. Dix, my duffel bag from Vietnam was finally located. My ring and dog tags had been recovered and sent to the church at Orleans since that was my home of record. I was glad to have my wedding ring back. The only thing I ended up losing was a Swiss Army knife. All my cash was even there although it was in military currency which wasn't negotiable. I had to get permission to convert the money back into dollars.

Throughout my military career one of my primary jobs was providing counseling to those young soldiers. Sometimes I dealt with spiritual issues, but sometimes I had to help them deal with other problems they were facing. Many were homesick and wanted to go AWOL. They had family issues and financial issues. They had problems with other soldiers or with their officers. Sometimes they wanted advice and sometimes they just wanted someone to listen to them.

I learned never to try to understand the Army. We had sixteen companies at Ft. Dix and several chaplains. They were starting to draw down troops, so they started moving people out, including most of the chaplains. Eventually we were down to two companies and just me as the chaplain. Then they decided to move the companies back in, but they didn't bring back the chaplains. That meant I became responsible for sixteen companies by myself.

One day a painter came from maintenance to paint the chapel. I knew he was only supposed to paint the offices, so I reminded him of that. He said, no, he was supposed to paint the whole chapel. Again, I told him he was only supposed to be the offices. He ignored me and painted the whole chapel. A few days later I heard that he had been chewed out for painting the whole chapel and had to reimburse the Army for the extra paint he had used without authorization.

In November of 1969, I was reassigned to Germany. We arrived in Giessen where I was assigned to an artillery unit. Our belongs didn't arrive for several weeks. We lived in temporary quarters for a few weeks waiting for permanent housing. The buildings were former German officer quarters. On the top floor were the maids' quarters which had become one huge apartment. We had eight bedrooms and multiple bathrooms and a very long hallway. The children enjoyed running up and down the hall and playing hide and seek in the empty rooms.

We hadn't bought a converter yet for our TV so we couldn't receive any English channels. I still remember how funny it was to watch *Gunsmoke* and hear Festus walk into the Long Branch Saloon and say, "Guten Tag!"

I was only in Germany a few weeks when I had to fly home for my father's funeral. I left on Friday and flew into Maguire Air Force Base in New Jersey. They said I could fly out more quickly if I went to North Carolina. Then I went to Atlanta and arrived around midnight. It was right before Christmas and the airport was packed with soldiers trying to get home. There was one last plane going to Louisville that evening. I took my orders to the ticket agent and he put the paperwork on the bottom of the pile. I thought there was no way I'd make the flight and I'd miss the funeral Saturday morning. However, they called my name first and I boarded the flight.

My brother picked me up and we made it to the funeral. On Sunday morning, I flew back to Maguire to get a plane back to Germany. They put me on a flight, and I arrived in Germany around 10 a.m. Monday morning. There used to be a rule that you couldn't go more than three hundred miles on a three-day pass, but I went about six thousand miles. I was charged two days leave and most people didn't even realize I had been gone. This was another time when God was watching over me and working things out so I could attend the funeral and be with my family.

That first Christmas in Germany was special. We didn't have most of our belongings, so I bought a little tree and made a stand out of a cardboard Coke box. The children made all the ornaments for the tree.

The assignment in Giessen was difficult because the war in Vietnam was still going on. Most of the supplies and resources were being sent there so there wasn't a lot to do.

After about a year I was transferred to Wiesbaden. The family stayed in the Air Force base housing. Since it was the Air Force Headquarters in Germany, there were some nice facilities for the family. We lived right across the street from the school.

I was assigned to Camp Pieri, a small Army post on top of a mountain. There were about a thousand soldiers in that artillery unit. That assignment was my most difficult one. The post was a mess. I didn't have any support from the commanding officer. He didn't care for chaplains. That impacted our attendance in services.

The Army realized that things were bad as well. I left one Friday and came in on Monday and found I was the ranking officer. All the senior officers including the commander had been pulled out and were eventually replaced.

One day, the captain came up to me and said they were going to have a change of command ceremony and didn't want it to rain. I asked what time the ceremony was going to take place. He said ten o'clock. I said, I'd see what I could do. I have no idea why he thought I could control the weather. The ceremony started about fifteen minutes late. About ten minutes after eleven it started to rain. Afterwards the captain came up to me all upset. He said it wasn't supposed to rain. I told him, "I did my job. It wasn't my fault you started late and didn't finish at eleven. Next time, you need to start on time." That's when I started telling people that I was in sales not in management.

There was a surge of terrorism in Germany and throughout Europe in the early 1970s. The Baader Meinhof gang was actively bombing cars, buildings and train stations. There was a lot of security on the base and there were frequent bomb threats.

Despite that, we were able to travel throughout Europe. We went through Switzerland, Austria, the Netherlands, Italy and Belgium. Pat and I took a weekend trip to Paris. We took advantage of our weekends to make sure the children learned the history and culture of Europe. That is something we wouldn't have been able to do without the Army.

Pat had always wanted to see the Vienna Woods. My daughter read a book about the Lipizzaner horses and wanted to see them. For our anniversary, we decided to take the whole family to Vienna. We went with another chaplain and his family. He made the hotel arrangements and was all excited that he found this great deal.

We arrived late in the evening and found our hotel. It turned out to a glorified campground. Our room had four bunkbeds with cement-like straw mattresses and pillows. A cold front came through and there was no heat. If you moved an inch you would hit a cold spot in the bed and wake up. Pat slept all huddled up with just her nose out of the covers.

We couldn't get to the Vienna Woods because of road construction. It was too dark to see the "Blue Danube". The Vienna Boys Choir was traveling and was in New York. We did manage to get tickets to see the horses perform. All they had left were two box seat tickets and standing tickets. We sent our wives off to the box seats and took all the children to the standing section.

About half-way through the performance, an earthquake struck. The huge chandelier over the riding field began to sway. People started to panic, but the horses kept right on performing. The tremor passed and the announcer calmed everyone down so the performance could continue.

It was not the anniversary trip I envisioned, but we always remembered it and would joke about it often.

My unit went down to Crete for training, which allowed me to visit Greece and see Athens. Every year the annual chaplain's training took place in Berchtesgaden in Bavaria. It used to be Hitler's headquarters, but the U.S. military took it over and used it for conferences and recreation. It was always nice to be able to bring the family there and travel around Salzburg and picturesque Bavaria.

I enjoyed meeting the German people. They were very welcoming.

As I mentioned, we arrived in Giessen right before Christmas. December 6th is St. Nicholas Day in Germany. German children put their shoes outside their door and St. Nicholas brings them candy if they are good or coal if they are bad. There were two German ladies in the building married to American soldiers. They knew none of our things had arrived. They told the children about the tradition. They surprised the children with beautiful gingerbread houses which "magically" appeared on the doorstep. Pat got sick for several weeks with pleurisy and those German ladies helped with the children.

In Wiesbaden the children had an older German couple who babysat for us. The children called them Oma and Opa, which meant grandmother and grandfather. Connie became very fluent in German and ended up studying the language in college.

Pat's father and stepmother were able to come visit us for two weeks and we took them around to several countries, including Switzerland and the Netherlands. They were thrilled to be able to come. Pat's uncle had been stationed in Germany for years and her dad had always wanted to see the places his brother talked about.

We stayed in Wiesbaden for two years. The Olympics were going to be held in Munich in 1972. We had planned a big trip to Scandinavia that summer and were also going to try and go to some of the events. They cut my tour short and sent me to New York for a ten-month officer's training course. That, of course, was the year the Israeli Olympic team members were killed. Even though we were disappointed, God was still watching over us.

The chaplain's school was in Ft. Hamilton, New York. It was in Brooklyn under the Verrazano Bridge. I was given the opportunity to go downtown to Long Island University in the evenings and weekends to work on my Masters' degree in counseling.

It was tough. I had military school from 8 a.m. to 4 p.m. After class, a group of us would take the subway downtown and go to LIU at night. Ten months later, though, I had my Masters' degree. Although I appreciated this opportunity to further my education at almost no expense, I missed holding services and working with the troops.

There were ninety-two chaplains taking the training course. There were three apartment buildings where all the families lived. There were about thirty families in each building.

One of the biggest scares of my life happened in that apartment building. Pat and a couple of the other wives were down in the basement putting some things in the storage unit. The children were all upstairs in one of the apartments playing. I and the other two men were in the elevator going to get some more things when the fire alarm went off and the elevator stopped. We could smell the smoke, but we were stuck. Our wives were in the basement and our children were upstairs alone and we couldn't do anything to help. Fortunately, it was a small fire that was put out quickly. When we got up to the children, they were all playing and having a good time. They never knew that anything had been wrong.

We took the opportunity to see some shows, visit museums and tour the city. Pat and I debated about whether to send the children to the public school in Brooklyn. Many of the chaplains were sending their children to private schools. We decided to keep them in the public schools. Connie was in sixth grade and Donald was in fourth grade. They did just fine. The school sponsored many field trips and the children were able to learn a great deal about New York City.

When I gave my life to God at twenty-two, I promised to go wherever He wanted me to go. I meant it when I told God to take my life and use it. However, I think God grants our petitions as well. There were four things I wanted to do while I was in the Army and I prayed and asked God to grant my requests. He graciously granted them all. I wanted to go to Europe, I wanted to serve the soldiers in Vietnam, I wanted to get some more schooling and I wanted to get the eight years of active duty I needed to retire from the reserves.

After I completed school, I was a major, but the Army was drawing down troops. I was told I had to leave active duty, but I could remain in the reserves. I never received a good explanation about why I had to leave. My age probably played a role. It didn't matter to me because I had completed the eight years I needed. God was calling me back to the civilian ministry.

Although I was leaving active duty and going back into the reserves, I found it was good to have the officer's course that I just finished. It helped me get my promotions down the road. I was able to network with a lot of chaplains. I keep in touch with some of them.

I remained in the reserves for the next fifteen years and was able to earn my promotion to lieutenant colonel and ultimately retired as a full colonel in 1987. I proudly served in the military for thirty-four years. There aren't many people who can say they started their career as a Navy Seaman Recruit and ended up an Army full Colonel.

Chapter Nine

Bunker Hill, Indiana

I was heading back to a civilian congregation, but I also wanted to keep a military congregation. One of the chaplains asked if I had a place to go. I said, "No, the Lord hasn't told me yet, but I know He has a place for me. He's been doing this all through my ministry. I'll be okay."

Shortly thereafter, I received a phone call from a church in Indiana. I wanted to take my thirty-day leave before I started working in a church and asked if they were willing to wait that long. I told them I could meet with them in August. August 5th was my anniversary and I ended up in Bunker Hill, Indiana talking with that church. It was in northern Indiana near Kokomo.

I moved the family back to Kentucky for the thirty days while I looked for a church. I had two churches that had talked to me, the one in Bunker Hill and one in Evansville. I called headquarters in Texas asking what reserve openings they had in Indiana. I was hoping it would help me pick the right church. They told me they had two spots, one in southern Indiana and one in Northern Indiana which didn't help.

I felt the Lord was calling me to Bunker Hill. It was a few miles from Grissom Air Force Base. There were a lot of air force families and retirees in the community. They had a commissary and exchange we could use.

I drove up and preached a trial sermon. They called me on Wednesday to say there had been a unanimous vote for me to come be their pastor. I accepted the position.

We had left all our furniture in New York. I called the movers to have my furniture shipped to Indiana. We arrived in Bunker Hill on a Thursday and I was told my furniture could be there by Saturday. I didn't realize they meant the next Saturday. We had ten days before our things arrived. We slept on sleeping bags. Some of the church members began thinking we didn't have any furniture.

This was the beginning of a new era. The Lord continued to work things out according to His plan. I had a reserve unit near the base about five miles from the church.

I had been in southern Indiana right out of seminary but hadn't spent much time in the north. We stayed at the church almost ten years.

It was a nice place for the children to grow up. By now, they were in fifth and seventh grade. Bunker Hill was a small town of about eight hundred people. That was a real change for the children since we were coming out of Brooklyn. They had always lived on large military bases, never in such a small town. There were a lot of young people their age in the church. They finally got to stay in a school more than just a year. They made lots of friends.

My son's elementary school was right across the street from the parsonage. The middle and high school were out in the country, but they were nice facilities. I think the children received a good education there. It was good for them to be settled in one spot.

Both the children became involved in the music programs at school. We took them all over the state for music competitions and for choir performances. Donald played baseball and tennis. He and his friends would ride their bikes out to the school in the summer to go swimming. The town was safe. He could leave in the morning and come home in the evening and you never had to worry about his safety.

Connie was in Girl Scouts and made some close friends that she still has contact with today. Bunker Hill became home for the whole family.

I had my twenty years of military service, but I was able to get nine more years with the reserve unit while I as at Bunker Hill. The church was supportive of my military service. I could continue ministering to the service men and women. Most of the time I had been on active duty with the Army, I was on posts right next to air bases. In Germany we had lived in Air Force housing. Now in Bunker Hill, we were the closest town to Grissom Air Force Base.

My reserve unit was a training unit again. Our headquarters was up in Michigan. I was responsible for a brigade, so I did have to travel to Fort Wayne, Indianapolis, Anderson and Bloomington. I used to drive to Indianapolis on Sunday morning for services. I'd have a 7:30 a.m. service and then drive an hour back to have a 10:00 a.m. service in Bunker Hill. I did that for about two years. On weekends I would sometimes put six or seven hundred miles on the car driving to the various units. Our two-week training periods took me all over the U.S. I enjoyed it, though, because I was still serving those young people.

The church wasn't large, but it was stable. Our attendance was about a hundred people. They worked together well and seemed to enjoy each other. We reached out to the families at the air base and many of them started coming to the church. I truly believed those families were missionaries. They would go out from our church when they got reassigned and I was always heartened when I would hear they were active in new congregations.

The congregation was very cooperative. There was a Sunday School class of seniors. I ended up baptizing five of them. Most of them were in their seventies. I had learned long never to assume that someone had given their heart to God just because they had been in the church for decades.

The church had a good mix of older people, families and children. The church supported missions. They were one of the top ten givers in the state to mission giving.

We were still close to family in Kentucky. We were about two hundred miles from them, but that was much closer than we had been since I joined the Army. We were able to spend Christmas with family which the children enjoyed. We bought a popup camper and continued our practice of traveling around the country on family vacations.

I became involved in some of the state and association activities which allowed me to network with some of the other ministers.

I have always been a strong believer in bringing the men of the church together for discipleship training. The women would always meet and have missionary circle meetings, but the men never seemed to meet as a group. We started a men's brotherhood ministry so the men would be more involved. Several of our men because officer's in the state brotherhood association.

At our first breakfast, one of the men who used to be an Army mess sergeant cooked a wonderful breakfast. Afterwards, when everyone was cleaning up, someone threw him a towel and asked him to dry the dishes. He replied that he cooked, he didn't do dishes. He was serious, but he continued to cook for every breakfast.

I encouraged the church to build an educational building which they needed to grow. That was one of their goals, but they just kept putting it off. I'd mention it occasionally and they would hem and haw. They had money in their building fund, but just kept collecting more. I finally told them, "if you aren't going to build the building, then you need to take the money out of that fund and give it to missions or some other ministry." That riled them up some, but they finally got it built.

To pay for the expansion, they were going to borrow money by taking out a thirty-year loan. They ended up getting a twenty-year loan which they paid off in nine years. There were a lot of farmers in the congregation who didn't like debt.

The parsonage was beautiful, but it only had two bedrooms. The church agreed to add a bedroom and a bathroom to the parsonage. Donald had been sleeping in my cramped little study.

The Lord was good to us by allowing us to serve in Bunker Hill. We stayed there until both the children graduated from high school. The church was having a hundred and forty or fifty people in Sunday services when we left.

Chapter Ten

Columbus, Indiana

I received a call from a church in Columbus, Indiana. The town was much larger than Bunker Hill with about thirty-five thousand people. It was in the southern part of the state closer to family in Kentucky. Columbus is the headquarters of Cummins Engine. It is famous for its modern architecture. There are over eighty building on their architectural tour. The head of Cummins loved modern architecture and he paid the architectural fees for most of the public buildings and churches in town.

I accepted the call to go to Memorial Baptist Church. I planned to stay there about ten years and then retire, if that was in the Lord's will. I had always liked the Columbus area. One of my friends had pastored that church before. The Lord granted me my wish. We started there in July of 1982 and I retired in June of 1992.

I still had a reserve unit for five more years. I was now a full colonel and they wouldn't let me stay at the unit in Bunker Hill because my rank was too high. Instead, I was assigned to DARCOM in Washington, DC. For several years I would go to Washington, DC for my two-week training. I would help plan the annual chaplains training meeting. For two years I was able to travel to some of the depots around the country and work with the other chaplains and hold services. I went to Redstone Arsenal in Alabama for two weeks. I helped the new commander and he wrote me a nice report about how I'd helped him out.

For a chaplain, colonel was pretty much the highest rank you could hold. There is one Chief of Chaplains and one Deputy Chief who are two- and one-star generals, respectively. I received a letter that I was eligible to be considered for the promotion to Chief. I was very honored. However, the current Chief was American Baptist and I knew they wouldn't replace him with another American Baptist Chaplain.

I wouldn't have wanted the position anyway because the work would involve politics and administration. It was an easy decision to not submit my application. I never wanted to do administrative work in the military. Despite retiring as a Colonel in 1987, I was blessed to be able to work with the troops almost my entire career

The congregation at Memorial was growing. Like almost every church I pastored, they needed more space. Their sanctuary seated about two hundred and fifty people, but they had no place to hold Sunday School or have fellowships for that many people. We needed more parking and expanded the parking lot. We finished up the basement with classroom space. We made the physical building ready to accommodate the growth we were confident the Lord would provide.

Throughout most of my ministry, I was involved in building projects. I know people can worship God anywhere. I experienced that in Vietnam. However, realistically, if people outside the church see that a church is neglected or cramped or not accessible because of stairs, no parking or poor lighting, it's hard to get them to come and hear God's Word. If the congregation doesn't care about God's house, why should someone from the outside want to come in.

Memorial didn't have a men's brotherhood group, so we started one. Just like in Bunker Hill, some of the men became very active and were state officers.

One of our members stopped coming and I went to talk to him to find out why. He said it was because the people weren't "spiritual" enough. I asked him what exactly he meant by that and to explain his definition of "spiritual." He didn't have any answer. I didn't expect him to. It was just another excuse for not going to church. He never did come back. Sometimes you just can't convince people, but I learned long ago that my job was to tell people about Christ. It was their place to receive or reject the Lord.

When I announced my retirement, the church was very supportive. God had given me a vision for the church, and I felt we accomplished that vision in the ten years I was there. It was time to retire and turn the church over to a younger pastor. Up until then, they hadn't had a pastor stay for more than four years, so my ten-year tenure was a record.

I once said I was surprised, they let me stay for ten years. One lady told me that they kept me because they wanted Pat to stay and knew if I left, she would go, too. I hope she was joking, but I know they all loved Pat.

The congregation held a beautiful retirement ceremony and reception for Pat and me. They sent invitations to all the churches I had pastored. I was touched that so many former members came to the retirement party. Pat had led choirs in many of the churches and she was able to direct a mass choir made up of members from all her past choirs. Some of Pat's family came. What was more surprising for me was that all my brothers and my sister came to the ceremony. That was the last time we were all together.

I didn't live my life looking for recognition, but that day my brothers finally came to appreciate that with God's help I had accomplished a great deal in my life and that I wasn't the little brother they never thought would amount to much.

Even though we left Memorial, Pat and I knew we wanted to stay in Columbus, so we bought our first house. We had always lived in either school housing, military housing or parsonages so it was a real change for us to have a home we owned. We were ready for the next step in our journey with God.

Chapter Eleven

Interim Pastor

When I gave up the church at Memorial, my plan wasn't to fully retire. Ever since seminary I had felt called to help smaller churches that couldn't afford a full-time pastor. I had prayed about it for many years and believed that God wanted me to retire at sixty-two while I was still young enough to serve these churches.

I became an interim pastor at twelve different churches. My job was to go in, identify any problems, try to resolve them, and get them ready for their new pastor. I believe that with God's help every church I turned over to a pastor was in better shape than when I arrived.

At one church, they thought I was too old to serve them. I was seventy-eight at the time. They didn't have a lot of choice, so they agreed to let me come. I worked with them for a year. There were a lot of teachers and educators in that church. I told them that if my grammar wasn't the greatest to chalk it up to my Kentucky roots. When I left, the deacons put a very nice letter in the local paper saying that I was a wonderful model of an interim pastor. I was there when they were sick and when they needed me, and they appreciated my service to them.

One church was in a mess. At a church social, one of the ladies asked me what an interim pastor did. I told her that I came to get this congregation back in the hands of the Lord. She was taken aback and said they already were. I replied that if they were, they wouldn't be in such a mess.

My next to last Sunday, I asked them to put a note on their refrigerator that read "This is God's church and it's where I worship." There was so much trouble with people who thought it was "their" church. They had their little kingdoms they tried to control. On the last Sunday, a woman who had been the biggest problem came forward and said, "I did what you said. I put that note on my refrigerator. I realize now that this is God's church."

So many people think the church is there to serve them and in some ways it does. However, God gave us gifts so we would serve the church. We are the hands and feet of the Body of Christ.

One church had been relatively large and built a large building. They still owed a substantial amount of money on the mortgage. Then they started having problems and people started leaving the church. Suddenly the handful of people who were left found themselves unable to make the monthly mortgage payments. They feared they would lose the building.

I prayed about the situation for months and then God showed me the solution. One Sunday I told them I knew how they could get rid of the debt. If thirty-seven people would contribute $2,700, they could have the building paid off in three months. I pledged to give the first $2,700. It took four months, but we got it paid off and relieved the burden they had been carrying. Even though I was an interim, I always believed that while I was serving a church, I was a part of it and needed to be part of finding the solutions to the problems.

A lady in another church told me one Sunday that their other interims and pastors always lectured them on what "they" needed to be doing. She appreciated that I always said "we" needed to do whatever it was. I believe that a successful pastor should be a partner with the congregation and work with them to fulfill God's mission and not just stand in the pulpit and point out their faults.

It is funny what people hear. One Sunday I was preaching a sermon on fulfilling your purpose. I made the statement that everything in creation had a purpose. Even a mosquito had a purpose. I also stated that all of creation knew its purpose. It was only man who didn't know his purpose. As I was standing at the door shaking hands with people on the way out, a man stopped and said he was upset with me. I asked him why and he said he was mad because I said he wasn't as smart as a mosquito.

Another church was planning to build. They had a lot of money in a building fund that had been sitting there for years. I told them that if God wanted them to build the building they needed to start. If He didn't want them to build it, they needed to do something more constructive with the money.

On the way out, one of the men stopped me. He said that they just didn't have the money to build that building and they needed to wait until they had more money before they started. I pointed out the cemetery next to the church and asked him what he thought would happen to him when he died. He said he guessed they'd bury him in the cemetery. I asked him if he thought he was going to heaven and he said yes. I told him that if he didn't think God could help them get that building built, how did he think God was going to raise him out of that cemetery into heaven. I think he got the point. If God wants you to do something, you need to step out on faith and do it. He will help. They eventually built the building.

At one of the churches there was a mischievous little boy who liked to play tricks on people. One morning I found a rubber snake on my chair on the platform during the morning service. I just picked it up and put it aside. I knew he had put it there. I didn't say anything about it which I know took some of the fun out of it for him. Pat and I went on a trip somewhere and I bought a rubber spider. A few Sundays later, as his family was walking out the door, I put that rubber spider in my hand and then shook his hand. He must have jumped a foot.

I love to tell humorous stories to illustrate my sermon points. One woman even wrote a book entitled, "Let Me Tell You a Story" as a sort of tribute to my preaching style.

I served one church for fourteen months. I told them that Pat and I wanted to drive to Alaska. At the end they kindly gave us a dinner and $3,000 for our trip. We were gone about six weeks. When we returned, I received a call from them again saying the new pastor had decided not to come so would I come back and be their interim pastor again. I stayed for another fourteen months until they called a new pastor. Then he became seriously ill and couldn't work for four months. I came back a third time cover for him until he was well enough to return.

I will confess to some envy. As I mentioned, my first church was at New Providence. It was a small, rural church outside of Scottsburg, Indiana. First Baptist Church of Scottsburg was the "big" church. I told Pat that one day I'd be the pastor there. The Lord let me pastor there twice as an interim. They had a radio ministry which was a first for me. I would often have people tell me they listened to me every week on the radio. That church was the last church I pastored.

At the age of eighty-four I stopped being an interim pastor. I started and ended my ministry in Scottsburg. All told, I had eighteen civilian churches and eight military congregations.

Some of the churches I pastored are still thriving, but several are not. I sometimes get discouraged and wonder whether I made any difference at all. Then I remember that Scripture in 1 Corinthians 3:7, *"I have planted, Apollos watered; but God gives the increase."* God planted me at each church for a specific purpose for a specific time. Until I get to Heaven, I will never know fully the influence I might have had, but that isn't for me to worry about. God asked me to serve Him faithfully and I believe I did. The rest is up to Him.

Chapter Twelve

The Journey Continues

After I stopped being an interim pastor, Pat and I were still in good health. My hearing was mostly gone because of the explosion I suffered in the Army. That had made it more and more difficult for me to pastor because I couldn't hear conversations. We had our aches and pains, but we were able to still travel. Pat was finally glad to be called by her name and not "the pastor's wife."

For our forty-fifth anniversary we went with Connie on our first cruise to England and Scandinavia. When I was younger, I had seen the movie, *The Song of Norway,* and always wanted to see Norway. We were unable to go to Scandinavia while we were in Germany because they cut my tour short.

Pat and I sold the popup trailer we had when the children were young and bought a thirty-foot camper and camped all over the United States for many years. When I first retired, we briefly thought about spending winters in Florida, but after trying it for six weeks that first year we decided that wasn't for us. Plus, it would have prevented me from serving as an interim which I felt God was calling me to do. Once Pat went on that first cruise, she didn't want to camp anymore. She decided hotels and cruises were more comfortable.

On our fiftieth anniversary, Donald and Connie joined us on a cruise to Alaska. On our sixtieth wedding anniversary, we went with Connie and her friend, Ginny, on a cruise to Australia and New Zealand. We would often travel to Maryland and Texas to visit Connie. We went to Florida for a week each winter. We took several more cruises. Together we went to more than thirty countries, all fifty states and all the Canadian provinces. Because of my military time, I went to over forty countries. I was so blessed that God allowed me to show my family His beautiful world.

We had never moved our membership from Memorial Baptist Church and returned there to worship after I stopped doing interim work. Pat was very active in the women's mission organization. I've been active in the men's brotherhood.

In April of 2018, Pat passed away suddenly. We would have celebrated our sixty-third wedding anniversary in August. That was a difficult week. I conducted the funeral services for my last brother, Bud, on Monday and Pat died on Saturday.

When Pat died, the people at Memorial fixed a lovely dinner after the funeral. Many of them came and sat with me and the children at the hospital. I greatly appreciated their love and support. People from many of the churches I pastored over the years came to her service as did many family members from all over the country.

My daughter, Connie, has come to live with me and we continue our travels. We drove fifty-four hundred miles through the west in August of 2018. It was fun going to Dodge City. I still love the show, *Gunsmoke*. Connie has a camper, so we've been doing some camping again.

Now we are spending the winter in Texas. I've been able to spend more time with both of my children since Pat died. We went up to Chicago with Donald to a Cubs game and have made more time to meet up with him for lunch or dinner.

I love to go bowling and have been in a bowling league for several years. Although my average has dropped, Connie and I have been practicing while we are in Texas. I had cataract surgery and praise God I'm now able to see without my glasses for the first time in years. I've made more time to visit my last remaining sister, Lil, who encouraged me to write this book.

I don't know where my journey will lead next, but I continue to trust God to guide me.

Chapter 13

Say Yes to God

I have been writing about my years of service to the church, to the military and most of all to the Lord. Now I've almost come to the end of my life. I'm eighty-eight. I don't have the military, I don't have a church and don't have role in the church now. I feel that I'm still healthy enough to be doing something for God.

There's a verse in Romans 8:28 that I love. It says, "*All things work together for the good for those who love God and are called according to His purpose.*" It doesn't say everything is good. It says He will make something good out of any situation. In my life I've seen Him make good things out of terrible situations.

When I lost my wife so suddenly, I kept asking myself what good is going to come out of it all. She was a child of God and very devoted pastor's wife. She was my rock and my support for sixty-two years. Now she's gone from this world. For her, everything is good. The cough and arthritis she suffered with for years is gone. She's with her Lord, but I'm left behind without her.

I'm wondering why I'm left here. I'm waiting to find out what the Lord's purpose is for me. When I was a teenager, I had no purpose and no direction. Right now, I'm at the same point of not knowing where I'm going. I hate to conclude this book on a negative note, but I need to be honest. I'm trying to find a new purpose.

I know it's there, but God hasn't revealed it to me yet. In a way it's exciting because I know God has something for me. As I said many years ago when I was coming back into the civilian ministry again, "I don't know where I'm going, but I know God has a plan for me." Now I'm waiting again to see what new adventure He has for me.

Looking back, many things in my life weren't good, but I saw how God worked and how He changed them into something good. This past year has reminded me of that lesson.

Two young soldiers gave their life taking me to that church service in Vietnam. I still think about them and feel thankful for them. Maybe they were saying "Yes, Lord." When I needed help and transportation they said "Yes, Lord." I continue to pray for their families. I pray they also saw something good come out of the sacrifice of their loved ones.

It's been a blessing to relive these experiences in this book and share what I've learned with those who might read it. Maybe this is the new way God is allowing me to serve. Through this book, maybe I can minister to people I can't physically reach anymore.

To whoever might read this I say, "Know one thing. God can take nothing and make something out of it. He can take that which seems to be of no value and make it valuable in His kingdom. He can take a life going nowhere and give it direction and a place of service." That's what He did for me.

When you look in the Bible you find that God always reached out to the lowly and to the common person to fulfill his purpose. He used a shepherd boy, a carpenter, a prostitute, a foreign woman, and a young, poor, virgin girl to fulfill his plan of redemption. They were the human ancestors of His Son.

Many years ago, He took a boy off the streets of Louisville and made a pastor out of him. He took an indifferent student who didn't think he could accomplish anything and allowed him to get several degrees so that he could become a better pastor and servant. I'm very grateful to Him for believing in me. It is humbling to know that the God of the universe wanted me to help build His Kingdom and shepherd His people.

Thinking about where I am, I can testify to how God has directed my life and blessed me. I hope if you read this book, if you haven't already, that you might say "Yes, Lord. I'll serve You." Then watch Him change your life. Amen.

ABOUT THE AUTHOR

Rev. Donald C. Humphrey has been a Baptist minister for almost sixty years and served as an Army Chaplain for twenty-four years. A veteran of the Vietnam War, he also served in the Naval Reserve for nine years. A native of Louisville, Kentucky, he graduated from Georgetown College, KY with a Bachelor of Arts degree majoring in History with a minor in Sociology. He received a Master of Divinity degree from Southern Theological Seminary and a Master of Science in Counseling from Long Island University. He was married to Patricia Bell for sixty-two years and has two children, Connie and Donald.

34233200R00070

Made in the USA
Lexington, KY
20 March 2019